AMAZONIANS SIMPLIFIED

AMAZONIANS SIMPLIFIED

SOLOMON HATHAWAY

Revitalized Occult and Strange

First Printing, 2024

Published by Revitalized Occult and Strange, an imprint
of Bald and Bonkers Network LLC

ISBN/SKU 979-8-3302-6071-3
EISBN 979-8-3302-6072-0

CONTENTS

CHAPTER 1

Introduction

In the rich tapestry of Greek mythology, the Amazons stand out as a formidable group of female warriors and hunters, renowned for their prowess in strength, agility, archery, and combat. They forged a society devoid of men, engaging with them solely for procreation, nurturing their daughters to follow in their footsteps, and entrusting their sons to the care of their fathers. Led by a valiant queen, these fierce and autonomous women embarked on extensive military campaigns, traversing territories from Scythia and Thrace to the expanses of Asia Minor, the Aegean archipelago, the deserts of Arabia, and the lands of Egypt.

Moreover, they are honored for establishing sacred temples and laying the foundations of venerable cities such as Ephesos and Smyrna.

The Amazons are believed to have resided on the fringes of the ancient world, with Pontus, located in the northern reaches of Anatolia by the Black Sea, often cited as their primary abode. It was from Themiscyra, perched on the banks of the Thermodon River, that their queen presided over their domain.

Palaephatus, an ancient writer, attempted to demystify Greek myths by proposing that the Amazons could have been men misidentified as women due to their attire and looks. His skepticism about their existence stemmed from the lack of evidence in his era. However, modern archaeological findings in the Eurasian Steppes have unearthed burial sites of female warriors, suggesting that the legendary Amazons may have been modeled after actual equestrian cultures such as the Scythians, Sarmatians, and Hittites. Notably, a 2019 discovery in Russia revealed a burial site containing generations of female Scythian warriors.

CHAPTER 2

Name

Etymology

The etymology of "Amazon" is ambiguous. It may derive from the Iranian term *ha-mazan*, signifying 'warriors,' as seen in the Persian verb "hamazakaran," which means 'to make war,' with the root *kar- denoting 'make.'

Another hypothesis suggests it originates from the Greek *n̥-mn̥gʷ-yō-nós, translating to 'man-less, without husbands,' a theory deemed improbable by scholar Hjalmar Frisk. Alternatively, it could stem from the Iranian *ama-janah, implying 'virility-killing.'

In ancient Greek belief, "Amazon" was thought to arise from ἀμαζός (amazos), meaning 'breastless,' composed of -a ('without') and mazos, a form of mastos ('breast'). This notion is linked to a tale, referenced by Marcus Justinus, about Amazons removing or cauterizing their right breast. Nonetheless, classical art contradicts this, portraying Amazons with both breasts, typically with one obscured. Philostratus mentioned that Amazon infants were not solely nourished from the right breast. The author Adrienne Mayor posits that this incorrect etymology may have fueled the legend.

Alternative terms

Herodotus referred to the Amazons using terms such as Androktones (Ἀνδροκτόνες), which translates to 'men killers' or 'husband slayers,' and Androleteirai (Ἀνδρολέτειραι), signifying 'men destroyers' or 'murderesses.' They were also known as Antianeirai (Ἀντιάνειραι), interpreted as 'equal to men.' Aeschylus, in his works, coined Styganor (Στυγάνωρ), meaning 'those who despise all men.'

In 'Prometheus Bound' and 'The Suppliants,' Aeschylus described the Amazons as 'the un-wed, flesh-devouring Amazons' (...τὰς ἀνάνδρους κρεοβόρους τ' Ἀμαζόνας). In the play 'Hippoly-tus,' Phaedra refers to Hippolytus as 'the son of the horse-loving Amazon' (...τῆς φιλίππου παῖς Ἀμαζόνος βοᾷ Ἱππόλυτος...). Nonnus, in 'Dionysi-aca,' names the Amazons of Dionysus An-drophonus (Ἀνδροφόνους), which means 'slayers of men.' According to Herodotus, the Scythians called the Amazons Oiorpata, a term derived from 'oior,' meaning 'man,' and 'pata,' meaning 'to slay.'

CHAPTER 3

Historiography

The belief in the existence of the Amazons, a race of warrior women from nomadic cultures, was not unique to the ancient Greeks. Similar stories were prevalent in the ancient civilizations of Egypt, Persia, India, and China. Greek mythology is replete with tales of encounters between Greek heroes and the formidable queens of this martial society. However, the precise location of the Amazons' homeland remained a mystery, often described as being in far-off, uncharted territories at the edge of the known world. For a long time, the Amazons were relegated to the realm of myth by scholars, though some hypothesized they might have been inspired by real groups. Theories suggested connections to societies in Asia Minor or Minoan Crete, with Lycia, Scythia, and Sarmatia being the most probable historical parallels, aligning with the narratives of Herodotus. In his 'Histories,' written in the 5th century BC, Herodotus recounted that the Sauromatae, ancestors of the Sarmatians and inhabitants of the region between the Caspian and Black Seas, were descendants of Amazons and Scythians.

Herodotus observed unique traditions among the Lycians in southwest Asia Minor, who adhered to matrilineal inheritance and social standing. They identified themselves by their mother's lineage, and an individual's social position was influenced by the mother's standing. This profound respect for women and the maternal line prompted Herodotus to speculate that the Lycians might have descended from the legendary Amazons.

Contemporary historiography has expanded beyond textual and artistic sources to include a wealth of archaeological findings from thousands of nomadic graves stretching from the Black Sea to

Mongolia. The unearthing of female remains bearing signs of combat and interred with weaponry such as bows, arrows, quivers, and spears, provides tangible evidence that warrior women did indeed exist, emerging from the equestrian cultures of the Scythians and Sarmatians.

CHAPTER 4

Mythology

Mythology states that Otrera, the inaugural queen of the Amazons, was a demigoddess, born from the union of Ares, the deity of war, and Harmonia, a nymph from the Akmonian Wood.

Historical accounts detail two notable encounters with Amazons prior to the Trojan War, dated before 1250 BC. In one account, the valiant Greek hero Bellerophon was challenged by Amazons in Lycia, dispatched by King Iobates who anticipated Bellerophon's demise. Contrary to expectations, Bellerophon emerged victorious. In a separate account, the youthful King Priam of Troy allied with the Phrygians in a fierce battle against the Amazons at the Sangarios River.

Amazons in the Trojan War:

Characters from the Amazonian myths are featured in Homer's epic, the Iliad, which is among the oldest extant texts in European history, dating back to approximately the 8th century BC. The now-lost Aethiopis, attributed to Arctinus of Miletus from the 6th century BC and part of the Epic Cycle of the Trojan War, recounts the involvement of an Amazon contingent under the command of Queen Penthesilea, a Thracian. After Hector's demise, Penthesilea and her forces allied with the Trojans, posing a significant challenge to the Greeks. Despite their initial struggles, the Greeks, aided by the legendary Achilles, ultimately prevailed. In a climactic duel, Achilles killed Penthesilea. Homer acknowledged the widespread familiarity with Amazonian legends throughout Greece and posited that the Amazons resided in or around Lycia, situated in Asia Minor, within the bounds of the Greek world.

The city of Troy is noted in the Iliad as the site where Myrine met her end. Subsequently recognized as an Amazonian queen, Myrine was chronicled by Diodorus in the 1st century BC as having led the Amazons in a conquest against the Atlantians, culminating in a decisive victory in the city of Cerne, which they subsequently destroyed.

In Scythia

The poet Bacchylides and the historian Herodotus, from the 6th and 5th centuries BC respectively, located the origin of the Amazons in Pontus, on the southern edge of the Black Sea. They identified Themiscyra as the capital, situated by the Thermodon River's banks, close to what is now the city of Terme. Herodotus narrates the tale of Amazons settling in Scythia after being captured by a Greek fleet. Overcoming their captors during a sea voyage, they landed on the Scythian shores. There, they obtained horses and made their home on the vast steppes stretching between the Caspian and Black Seas. Over time, these Amazons merged with the Scythian people, giving rise to the Sauromatae, the ancestors of the Sarmatians.

Amazon Homeland

Strabo, a historian from the 1st century BC, visited and confirmed that the original homeland of the Amazons was located on the plains near the Thermodon River. However, by the time of his visit, the Amazons had long disappeared and were believed to have retreated into the mountains. Strabo noted that other writers, including Metrodorus of Scepsis and Hypsicrates, suggested that after leaving Themiscyra, the Amazons resettled beyond the territory of the Gargareans, an all-male tribe native to the northern foothills of the Caucasian Mountains. According to this account, the Amazons and Gargareans maintained a tradition for many generations where they met in secret once a year for two months in spring to conceive children. These encounters followed ancient tribal customs and involved collective sacrifices. Female offspring remained with the Amazons, while male children were returned to the Gargareans.

In the 5th century BC, the poet Magnes praised the bravery of the Lydians in a cavalry battle against the Amazons.

Heracles Myth:

Hippolyte, an Amazon queen, was slain by Heracles as he sought to obtain her magical belt, part of his Labours. The conflict escalated unintentionally, resulting in Heracles killing the queen and several other Amazons. Eventually, impressed by Heracles' strength, the Amazons relinquished the belt to him. In another version, Heracles does not kill Hippolyte but instead exchanges her kidnapped sister, Melanippe, for the belt.

Theseus Myth:

Queen Hippolyte (or Antiope, in some versions), abducted by Theseus, was taken to Athens where she married him and bore a son, Hippolytus. In retaliation, the Amazons invaded Greece, pillaging coastal cities of Attica and besieging Athens. According to another account, Hippolyte fought on Athens' side and perished alongside all the Amazons during the final battle.

Amazons and Dionysus:

Plutarch recounts that Dionysus and his

companions battled Amazons at Ephesus. The Amazons fled to Samos, pursued by Dionysus, who inflicted heavy casualties upon them at a place known as Panaema, the "blood-soaked field." Eusebius, a Christian author, mentions that during the reign of Oxyntes, mythical king of Athens, the Amazons destroyed the temple at Ephesus.

In another myth, Dionysus allies with the Amazons against Cronus and the Titans. Polyaenus writes that after Dionysus conquers the Indians, he enlists the Amazons in his service, using them in campaigns against the Bactrians. Nonnus, in his Dionysiaca, describes Amazons loyal to Dionysus, although they are noted not to originate from the Thermodon region.

Amazons in Relation to Alexander the Great

Biographers of Alexander the Great mention the Amazons, recounting a tale from the Alexander Romance where Queen Thalestris purportedly bore him a child. However, other biographers, including the respected Plutarch, dispute this claim.

Plutarch notes an instance when Alexander's naval commander Onesicritus read a passage about Amazons from his Alexander History to King Lysimachus of Thrace, who had participated in the original expedition. The king responded with amusement, asking, "And where was I then?".

According to the Talmud, Alexander considered conquering a "kingdom of women" but reconsidered when the women warned him: "If you kill us, people will say: Alexander kills women; and if we kill you, people will say: Alexander is the king whom women killed in battle."

Roman and Ancient Egyptian References

Virgil's depiction of the Volsci warrior maiden Camilla in the Aeneid draws from Amazon myths. Philostratus, in Heroica, writes of Mysian women who fought on horseback alongside men, similar to the Amazons. Their leader, Hiera, was the wife of Telephus. Legend also speaks of an Amazon expedition against the Island of Leuke, where Achilles' ashes were placed by Thetis. The ghost of Achilles frightened the horses so much that they threw off and trampled the invaders, forcing them to retreat. Virgil mentions the Amazons and their queen Penthesilea in his epic Aeneid (around 20 BC).

In his work De vita Caesarum, biographer Suetonius quotes Julius Caesar as stating that the Amazons once ruled a significant portion of Asia. Appian vividly describes Themiscyra and its defenses during Lucius Licinius Lucullus' Siege of Themiscyra in 71 BC, part of the Third Mithridatic War.

An Amazon myth survives in fragmented versions from 7th century BC Egypt. According to these accounts, the Egyptian prince Petechonsis and Assyrian troops launched a joint campaign into the Land of Women, near the Middle East border with India. Initially at odds with the Amazons, Petechonsis eventually fell in love with their queen, Sarpot, and allied with her against an invading Indian army. This story is believed to have originated independently in Egypt, separate from Greek influences.

Queens of the Amazons

Historical sources record names of individual Amazons who were regarded as queens and leaders of their people, often heading dynasties without male companions. They commanded armies of female warriors. Some of the most notable Amazon queens include:

- Otrera, daughter of the nymph Harmonia and the god of war, Ares. She is known as the mother of Hippolyta, Antiope, Melanippe, and Penthesilea, and is credited as the legendary founder of the Temple of Artemis in Ephesus.
- Hippolyta, daughter of Otrera and Ares. She features prominently in myths involving Theseus and Heracles, with Antiope as her sister. Alcippe, the only Amazon known to have taken a vow of chastity, was part of her retinue.
- Penthesilea, who accidentally kills her sister Hippolyta while hunting, later aids the besieged Trojans with her warriors. She is famously defeated by Achilles, who mourns her death.

- Lampedo and Marpesia, mentioned by Justin as queens of the Amazons.

- Myrina, who leads military expeditions in Libya, defeats the Atlanteans, allies with the ruler of Egypt, and conquers numerous cities and islands.

- Thalestris, the last known Amazon queen. Legend has it that she met Alexander the Great around 330 BC. Her homeland is identified as the region of Thermodon, or sometimes referred to as the Gates of Alexander, south of the Caspian Sea.

CHAPTER 5

Various Authors and Chroniclers

Quintus Smyrnaeus, in his work Posthomerica, details the attendants of Penthesilea, listing warriors such as Clonie, Polemusa, Derinoe, Evandre, Antandre, Bremusa, Hippothoe, Harmothoe with dark eyes, Alcibie, Derimacheia, Antibrote, and Thermodosa, all renowned for their prowess with the spear.

Diodorus Siculus recounts twelve Amazons who confronted and perished fighting Heracles in his quest for Hippolyta's girdle: Aella, Philippis, Prothoe, Eriboea, Celaeno, Eurybia, Phoebe,

Deianeira, Asteria, Marpe, Tecmessa, and Alcippe. After Alcippe's death, they launched a collective attack. Diodorus also mentions Melanippe, whom Heracles released after accepting her girdle, and Antiope as part of the ransom.

Diodorus lists another group led by Queen Myrina, who commanded the Amazons in a military campaign in Libya. She named the city of Mytilene after her sister Mytilene and named three more cities—Cyme, Pitane, and Priene—after other prominent Amazons who served under her.

Justin and Paulus Orosius, in their respective works, provide similar accounts of the Amazons. They mention queens Marpesia and Lampedo sharing power during incursions into Europe and Asia, where they met their demise. Marpesia's daughter Orithyia succeeded them, renowned for her military prowess. Orithyia shared power with her sister Antiope, who was away at war when Heracles attacked. Two of Antiope's sisters were captured—Melanippe by Heracles and Hippolyta by Theseus. Heracles later returned Melanippe to Antiope after receiving the queen's weapons in exchange, though some accounts suggest Melanippe was killed by Telamon. They also recount Penthesilea's role in the Trojan War.

In Hyginus' Fabulae, there is another list of names associated with the Amazons. Alongside Hippolyta, Otrera, Antiope, and Penthesilea, the list includes: Ocyale, Dioxippe, Iphinome, Xanthe, Hippothoe, Laomache, Glauce, Agave, Theseis, Clymene, and Polydora.

One of the most notable figures is Queen Otrera, who was married to Ares and mothered Hippolyta and Penthesilea by him]. She is also recognized for constructing a temple dedicated to Artemis in Ephesus .

In Valerius Flaccus' Argonautica, a different set of names is mentioned. He includes Euryale, Harpe, Lyce, Menippe, and Thoe. Among them, Lyce is noted in a fragment from the Latin Anthology, where she is credited with killing Clonus of Moesia, son of Doryclus, using her javelin.

CHAPTER 6

Late Antiquity, Middle Age and Renaissance literature

Stephanus of Byzantium, a 7th-century CE writer, offers various lists of the Amazons, with a particular emphasis on those who fell in battle against Heracles, whom he regards as their most illustrious member. Stephanus, along with Eustathius, links these Amazons to the place name Thibais, believed to be derived from an Amazon named Thiba. Stephanus credits the Amazons with founding several cities in Asia Minor, including Cyme, Smyrna, and Amastris—the latter supposedly named after an Amazon, despite actually being named for the historical figure Amastris. Similarly, the city of Anaea in Caria is said to be named after an Amazon.

Jordanes, in his mid-6th-century CE work 'Getica,' claims that the Goths, descendants of Magog, originated in Scythia near the Sea of Azov, situated between the Dnieper and Don Rivers. According to him, during a confrontation with Pharaoh Vesosis, Gothic women defended their territory against a neighboring tribe, leading them to establish their own military force under Marpesia's command. They crossed the Don River and embarked on an eastward conquest through Asia, subjugating regions including Armenia, Syria, and the entirety of Asia Minor, extending their reach to Ionia and Aeolis, and maintaining control over these lands for a century.

In the medieval epic Digenes Akritas, set in the 12th century and focusing on the Byzantine frontier, the protagonist battles and later engages in adultery with the female warrior Maximo, who is descended from Amazons taken by Alexander the Great from the Brahmans. The epic recounts various adventures involving these Amazonian descendants.

John Tzetzes, in his work Posthomerica, lists twenty Amazons who fell at Troy. This detailed list includes names like Toxophone, Toxoanassa, Gortyessa, Iodoce, Pharetre, Andro, Ioxeia, Oistrophe, Androdaixa, Aspidocharme, Enchesimargos, Cnemis, Thorece, Chalcaor, Eurylophe, Hecate, and Anchimache, among others.

In his book, the famous medieval traveler John Mandeville mentions the land of Amazonia, known as Feminye, where only women live without any men among them, not because men cannot live there, but because the women do not allow men to rule over them.

During the Medieval and Renaissance periods, authors credited the Amazons with inventing the battle-axe, possibly linked to the sagaris, an axe-like weapon associated with both Amazons and Scythian tribes in Greek literature. This attribution was initially met with surprise by authors like Paulus

Hector Mair, who considered it remarkable that such a "manly weapon" would be associated with a tribe of women, yet he accepted it based on authoritative sources like Johannes Aventinus.

Ariosto's Orlando Furioso features a nation of warrior women ruled by Queen Orontea, whose origin mirrors that of Greek myth, where abandoned women formed their own society to prevent men from regaining power. References to the Amazons and Queen Hippolyta also appear in Geoffrey Chaucer's Canterbury Tales, particularly in "The Knight's Tale."

During the European Renaissance, the debate about the historical reality of the Amazons continued, spurred on by accounts from explorers during the Age of Exploration. In 1542, Francisco de Orellana encountered and fought what he claimed were warlike women from the Icamiabas tribe on the Nhamundá River, a tributary of the Amazon. This encounter led to the naming of the Amazon River and the region of Amazonia in Portuguese and Spanish after these legendary women. Amazons also feature in the accounts of Christopher Columbus and Walter Raleigh.

CHAPTER 7

Names of Known Amazons

Labours of Heracles

In the tales of Heracles and his twelve labors, various Amazons are mentioned as being slain by him. These include Alcippe, Asteria, Celaeno, Deianira, Eriboea, and Tecmessa. Others, such as Aella and Pantariste, fought against Heracles but survived.

Trojan War

In John Tzetzes' "Posthomerica," a list is given of Amazons who accompanied Queen Penthesilea to the Trojan War and met their demise in battle. These Amazons are: Anchimache, Andro,

Androdaixa, Antianeira, Aspidocharme, Chalcaor, Cnemis, Enchesimargos, Eurylophe, Gortyessa, Iodoce, Ioxeia, Oistrophe, Pharetre, Thorece, Toxoanassa, and Toxophone.

Quintus Smyrnaeus, also in his "Posthomerica," lists the companions of Penthesilea at Troy who were killed by Greek warriors. Achilles slew Antandre, Antibrote, Harmothoe, Hippothoe, and Polemusa; Diomedes killed Alcibie and Derimacheia; Idomeneus of Crete killed Bremusa; Podarces killed Clonie after she had slain his comrade Menippus; Ajax the Lesser killed Derinoe after she had slain Laogonus; and Meriones killed Evandre and Thermodosa.

Other Named Amazons

- Agave
- Alke
- Dioxippe
- Euryale
- Glauce
- Lysippe
- Melanippe

- Menippe
- Molpadia
- Mytilene
- Xanthe

CHAPTER 8

Amazons in Art

Beginning around 550 BC, artistic representations of Amazons began to appear, portraying them as valiant warriors and adept horsewomen on vases. The motif of Amazonomachy, which depicts the conflict with the Amazons, gained popularity in pottery after the Battle of Marathon in 490 BC. By the 6th century BC, both public and private art frequently showcased images of Amazons on pediment reliefs, sarcophagi, mosaics, pottery, jewelry, and large-scale sculptures, embellishing prominent structures such as the Parthenon in Athens. This focus on Amazonian themes persisted into the Roman Imperial era and well into Late Antiquity.

The artistic portrayal of Amazons, with their embodiment of fierce femininity juxtaposed against male counterparts, extends beyond mere representation to reflect broader societal dynamics, both constructive and adverse. In Greek and Roman cultures, Amazonian myths served as a narrative and visual instrument to foster unity in the face of an external enemy. These mythical figures also represented various elements of the natural world and religious ideologies. Esteemed Roman authors like Virgil, Strabo, Pliny the Elder, Curtius, Plutarch, Arrian, and Pausanias invoked Amazonian lore to delve into the roots and identity of the Roman populace. Nonetheless, the depiction of Amazons in Roman narratives and artistry exhibited a vast spectrum—they were depicted alternately as allies of Troy, divine warriors, native Latins, belligerent Celts, noble Sarmatians, fervent Thracian monarchs, subdued Asians, or formidable opponents of Rome.

During the Renaissance in Europe, artists reinterpreted the Amazons within a Christian moral framework. Queen Elizabeth I of England was likened to an Amazonian warrior, symbolizing early feminist ideals. In "Divina Virago," Winfried Schleiner acknowledges Celeste T. Wright's observation of the Amazons' tarnished reputation during this era. The comparison of Elizabeth I to an Amazon is scarcely documented, likely due to the era's disapproval of the empowerment of women, which Amazons represented. Nevertheless, in 1565, Elizabeth I was present at a Westminster Palace tournament where men donned Amazon attire, signifying their emblematic presence in knightly rituals. Baroque and Rococo artists such as Peter Paul Rubens, Jan Brueghel, and Johann Georg Platzer vividly portrayed the Battle of the Amazons. Anselm Feuerbach, a 19th-century German Romantic artist, delved into Amazonian motifs, inspiring Romantics to seek the surmounting of personal and national limits through glorified retrospections.

CHAPTER 9

Archaeology

The hypothesis that Amazons have a historical foundation gains support from archaeological discoveries at kurgan burial sites in the southern Ukrainian and Russian steppes. The unearthing of varied weapons and artifacts in the graves of distinguished Scythian and Sarmatian female warriors suggests that the Amazonian legend could be rooted in actual practices. In areas such as the lower Don and lower Volga, about 20% of warrior graves contained women outfitted for combat, dressed similarly to men. In Sarmatian military burials, this figure rose to 25%. Vera Kovalevskaya, a Russian archaeologist, posits that Scythian women were compelled to defend themselves, their animals, and their lands with proficiency during periods when the men were engaged in warfare or hunting.

In the realm of early 20th-century Minoan archaeology, Lewis Richard Farnell and John Myres advanced a theory linking the Amazons' origins to the Minoan civilization. Myres, interpreting the tradition through the lens of alleged Amazonian cults, noted substantial similarities, suggesting a possible inception within Minoan society.

CHAPTER 10

Modern Influences

In Samsun Province, Turkey, the city of Samsun is home to an Amazon Village museum, which serves to celebrate the Amazons' heritage and foster both scholarly interest and tourism. The Terme district commemorates this legacy annually with the Amazon Celebration Festival.

The women of Mani were dubbed 'The Amazons of Diros' in 1826 after their victory over the Ottoman forces at the Battle of Diros during the Ottoman-Egyptian invasion of Mani.

Between 1936 and 1939, Nazi Germany

organized the Night of the Amazons (Nacht der Amazonen) annually at the Nymphenburg Palace Park in Munich. These events, which were part of the International Horse Racing Week Munich-Riem, showcased performances by bare-breasted entertainers from the SS-Cavalry. With 2,500 participants and guests from around the world, the events were designed to project an image of liberated women and a cosmopolitan, welcoming Nazi regime.

LITERATURE AND MEDIA:

Literature:

- Queen Hippolyta of the Amazons appears in William Shakespeare's plays A Midsummer Night's Dream and The Two Noble Kinsmen.

- Heinrich von Kleist's 1808 drama Penthesilea centers on the Amazon queen Penthesilea and her passionate nature.

- Steven Pressfield's 2002 novel Last of the Amazons reimagines the myth surrounding Theseus' abduction of Queen Antiope and the Amazons' attack on Athens, portraying the Archaic Greek world vividly.

- William Moulton Marston, alongside his wife Elizabeth Holloway and their lover Olive Byrne, created the Amazonian superheroine Wonder Woman for DC Comics. Marston's portrayal of the Amazons depicted them as physically and technologically superior beings.

- In Rick Riordan's The Heroes of Olympus series, the Amazons appear in The Son of Neptune and The Blood of Olympus, founding the Amazon corporation.

- Philip Armstrong's historical-fantasy series, The Chronicles of Tupiluliuma, features the Amazons as the Am'azzi.

- In Stieg Larsson's novel The Girl Who Kicked the Hornets' Nest, the Amazons are referenced as a transitional topic between sections of the book.

- Garci Rodríguez de Montalvo introduced the fictional queen Calafia, who ruled over a kingdom of black women styled after the Amazons, on the mythical Island of California.

- Amazon Gazonga, a short comic series created by the Waltrip brothers in 1995, centers on a young Amazon named Gazonga living in the Amazon rainforest.

- GastroPhobia, a webcomic by Daisy McGuire,

follows the adventures of an exiled Amazon warrior and her son in Ancient Greece approximately 3408 years ago.

Film and Television:

- The Kazakhstani film studio "Kazakhfilm" released the film Томирис (Tomyris) in late 2019, featuring the Amazon queen Tomyris portrayed by Almira Tursyn.

- Various Tarzan releases have included Amazon tribes, such as Tarzan and the Amazons and Tarzan, Lord of the Jungle.

- In the animated series The Mysterious Cities of Gold, a tribe of Amazons appears in two episodes.

- Frank Hart is kidnapped by Amazons portraying a misogynist in the 1980 film 9 to 5 [93].

- Amazons feature prominently in several movies including The Loves of Hercules (1960), Battle of the Amazons (1970), War Goddess (1973), Hundra (1983), Amazons (1986), Deathstalker II (1987), Ronal the Barbarian (2011), Hercules (2014), and DC Extended Universe films: Wonder Woman (2017), Justice League (2017), Wonder

Woman 1984 (2020), Zack Snyder's Justice League (2021).

- Amazons are also depicted in television series such as Hercules: The Legendary Journeys, Young Hercules, Xena: Warrior Princess, The Legend of the Hidden City, Huntik: Secrets & Seekers, and Supernatural.

Games:

- Amazons are featured in various role-playing and video games including Diablo, Heroes Unlimited, Aliens Unlimited, Amazon: Guardians of Eden, Flight of the Amazon Queen, A Total War Saga: Troy, Rome: Total War, Final Fantasy IV, Age of Wonders: Planetfall, Legend of Zelda series, and Yu-Gi-Oh games.

Military Units:

- In 1787, Russian general and statesman Grigory Potemkin, a favorite of Catherine the Great, established an Amazons Company. This company comprised wives and daughters of soldiers from the Greek Battalion of Balaklava.

- The Mino, or Minon (Our Mothers), constituted an all-female official military regiment in the late 19th to early 20th century in the former Kingdom of Dahomey (present-day Benin). Initially, women joined the army during deployments to bolster numbers, but their courage and effectiveness in combat led to the establishment of a regular unit. Western observers, noting certain Amazon-like physical and mental qualities, dubbed them the Dahomey Amazons.

Social and Religious Activism:

- From 1905 to 1913, members of the militant Suffragette movement were often referred to as "Amazons" in books and newspaper articles [95].

- In Ukraine, Katerina Tarnovska leads a group known as the Asgarda, claiming to be a modern tribe of Amazons. Tarnovska believes that Amazons are the direct ancestors of Ukrainian women and has developed an all-female martial art based on Combat Hopak, emphasizing self-defense.

Science:

- The Neptune Trojans, asteroids located 60° ahead or behind Neptune on its orbit, are individually named after mythological Amazons.

REFERENCES

- Diodorus Siculus, *Bibliotheca historica* 4.16.2
- Tzetzes, John, *Posthomerica* 179-182 (translated by Ana Untila)
- Quintus Smyrnaeus, *Posthomerica* [1]
- *Realencyclopädie der Classischen Altertumswissenschaft*. Band II, Halbband 3, *Apollon-Artemis* (1895): s. 681, s. v. *Areto*
- Blok, Josine H. *The Early Amazons: Modern and Ancient Perspectives on a Persistent Myth*. BRILL, 1995; page 218 (with a reference to *Lexicon Iconographicum Mythologiae Classicae*, "Amazones" entry, vol. 1, p. 653)
- Wilhelm Heinrich Roscher (ed.): *Ausführliches Lexikon der griechischen und

römischen Mythologie*. Band 2.1 (I-K), Leipzig, 1890–1894, p. 1429

- Wilhelm Heinrich Roscher (ed.): *Ausführliches Lexikon der griechischen und römischen Mythologie*. Band VI (U-Z), Hildesheim, 1965, s. 518
- Silver, Carly (July 29, 2019). "The Amazons Were More Than A Myth: Archaeological And Written Evidence For The Ancient Warrior Women". ATI. Archived from the original on January 12, 2021. Retrieved January 10, 2021.
- Adrienne Mayor (September 22, 2014). *The Amazons: Lives and Legends of Warrior Women across the Ancient World*. Princeton University Press. ISBN 9780691147208. Retrieved January 12, 2021.
- Carlos Parada, Maicar Förlag. "AMAZONS". maicar. Retrieved January 8, 2021.
- Andreas David Mordtmann. "Die Amazonen : ein Beitrag zur unbefangenen Prüfung und Würdigung der ältesten Überlieferungen". Reader digitale sammlungen. Retrieved January 8, 2021.
- Ian Harvey (August 5, 2019). "The Fierce

Amazon Warrior Women – What's Real and What's Myth". Vintage news. Retrieved January 10, 2021.

- Cartwright, Mark (November 14, 2019). "Amazon Women". World History Encyclopedia. Archived from the original on Apr 10, 2021. Retrieved January 8, 2021.
- Jacob Stern (1 January 1996). *On Unbelievable Tales*. Bolchazy-Carducci Publishers. ISBN 978-0-86516-320-1.
- Hansen, William F. (26 April 2005). *Classical Mythology: A Guide to the Mythical World of the Greeks and Romans*. Oxford University Press. ISBN 9780195300352 – via Google Books.
- Anton Westermann (1839). *Paradoxographoi [romanized]*.: Scriptores rerum mirabilium graeci. Insunt (Aristotelis) Mirabiles auscultationes; Antigoni, Apollonii, Phlegontis Historiae mirabiles, Michaelis Pselli Lectiones mirabiles, reliquorum eiusdem generis scriptorum deperditorum fragmenta. Accedunt Phlegontis Macrobii et Olympiadum reliquiae et anonymi tractus

De mulieribus, etc. sumptum fecit G. Westermann.

- Simon, Worrall (October 28, 2014). "Amazon Warriors Did Indeed Fight and Die Like Men". National Geographic. Archived from the original on Sep 20, 2016. Retrieved 13 September 2016.
- Foreman, Amanda (April 2014). "The Amazon Women: Is There Any Truth Behind the Myth?". Smithsonian. Smithsonian Institution. Archived from the original on Sep 9, 2016. Retrieved 14 September 2016.
- Schuster, Ruth (2 January 2020). "Tomb with Three Generations of 'Amazon' Warrior Women Found in Russia". Haaretz.
- J. H. Blok (1995). *The Early Amazons: Modern and Ancient Perspectives on a Persistent Myth*. BRILL. ISBN 90-04-10077-6.
- Hinge 2005, pp. 94–98
- "amazon | Etymology, origin and meaning of the name amazon by etymonline". www.etymonline.com. Retrieved 2023-11-13.
- Marylene Patou-mathis (1 October 2020). *L'homme préhistorique est aussi une

femme*. Allary éditions. pp. 313–. ISBN 978-2-37073-342-9.

- Haynes, Natalie (16 October 2014). "The Amazons: Lives & Legends of Warrior Women Across the Ancient World by Adrienne Mayor, book review". The Independent. Archived from the original on 2014-10-20. Retrieved 6 April 2015.
- One or more of the preceding sentences incorporates text from a publication now in the public domain: Chisholm, Hugh, ed. (1911). "Amazons". *Encyclopædia Britannica*. Vol. 1 (11th ed.). Cambridge University Press. pp. 790–791.
- Flavius Philostratus, Ellen Bradshaw Aitken, Jennifer K. Berenson Maclean (August 5, 2019). "Flavius Philostratus, On Heroes". The Center for Hellenic Studies. Archived from the original on January 26, 2021. Retrieved January 10, 2021.
- "The Amazons - Adrienne Mayor". BBC Radio Four. 6 April 2015.
- Aeschylus, *Prometheus Bound*.
- "Διονυσιακά/36 - Βικιθήκη". el.wikisource.org.

- Aeschylus, *Suppliant Women*.
- "The Amazons existed outside the range of normal human experience": P. Walcot (1984). "Greek Attitudes towards Women: The Mythological Evidence". *Greece & Rome*. 31 (1). jstor: 37–47. doi:10.1017/S001738350002787X. JSTOR 642368. S2CID 163008170. Retrieved February 2, 2021.
- M. Cyrino; M. Safran (8 April 2015). *Classical Myth on Screen*. Springer. pp. 179–. ISBN 978-1-137-48603-5.
- Herodotus, *The Histories*, p. 1.173.1.
- John Man (October 23, 2017). "The real Amazons: how the legendary warrior women inspired fighters and feminists". BBC History Magazine. Retrieved February 4, 2021.
- Simon Worrall (October 28, 2014). "Amazon Warriors Did Indeed Fight and Die Like Men". National Geographic. Archived from the original on October 19, 2019. Retrieved February 4, 2021.
- "HARMONIA". Theoi. Retrieved January 14, 2021.

- "ARES FAMILY - Greek Mythology". theoi com. Retrieved January 8, 2021.
- Adrienne Mayor, Josiah Ober (20 April 2018). "AMAZONS". Historynet. Retrieved January 8, 2021.
- Colin Quartermain (February 2, 2017). "BELLEROPHON IN GREEK MYTHOLOGY - Bellerophon and the Amazons". Greek legends and myths. Retrieved February 1, 2021.
- "Epic Cycle". Livius org. Retrieved January 13, 2021.
- Homer, *Iliad*, p. 2.45–46.
- Homer, *Iliad*, p. 3.52–55.
- Bruce Robert Magee. "The Amazon Myth in Western Literature". Louisiana State University and Agricultural & Mechanical College. Retrieved February 1, 2021.
- Herodotus, *The Histories*, p. 4.110.1.
- "Reading on Amazons". University of Washington. Retrieved January 13, 2021.
- "Suda Encyclopedia". Topostext. Retrieved February 1, 2021.
- Sue Blundell; Susan Blundell (1995).

Women in Ancient Greece p. 60. Harvard University Press. ISBN 978-0-674-95473-1.

- Stéphane Gsell. "Boston 98.916 (Vase), from the Vulci necropolis". Tufts University. Retrieved February 4, 2021.
- Tobias Fischer-Hansen; Birte Poulsen (2009). *From Artemis to Diana: The Goddess of Man and Beast*. Museum Tusculanum Press. pp. 333–. ISBN 978-87-635-0788-2.
- Page duBois (July 30, 1991). "Sappho Is Burning". University of Chicago Press. pp. 127–. ISBN 978-0-226-16772-1.
- "Ancient Amazons lived in the south of Ukraine – a historian". UKRAINE THE HISTORY OF THE STATE. 16 August 2019. Retrieved February 4, 2021.
- "The Amazon myth reflects the expectations of the Greeks". Pleiades. 16 August 2019. Retrieved February 4, 2021.
- "The Amazons". Monmouth College. 16 August 2019. Retrieved February 4, 2021.
- "The Amazons of Greek mythology are more than just a myth: The Amazons have left an archaeological and written record of the

ancient warrior women's past". ARCHYDE. 16 August 2019. Retrieved February 4, 2021.

- Mordtmann, Andreas David (1882). "Die Amazonen : ein Beitrag zur unbefangenen Prüfung und Würdigung der ältesten Überlieferungen". UB Heidelberg.

- A. David Mordtmann (1882). *Die Amazonen: ein Beitrag zur unbefangenen Prüfung und Würdigung der ältesten Überlieferungen*. Heidelberg University.

- H. Schneider (1860). *Trojanische Alterthümer. Zweiter Band. Die Sagen vom trojanischen Kriege, die Troas, die Amazonen, die Inschriften*. Bonn, Leipzig.

- Alexander Wilhelm Schlegel, Otto Wilhelm (1829). *The Amazons in Greek history and tradition: A manual of the mythology of the Greeks*. Göttingen.

- The Amazons in Greek history and tradition. G. de Bures. (1829).

- G. de Bures (1829). The Amazons in Greek history and tradition: A manual of the mythology of the Greeks. Goettingen.